St. Jerome Grade 4 Lesson Plan

St. Jerome Library

WWW.STJEROMELIBRARY.ORG

COPYRIGHT ©2021AD-2024AD BY ST. JEROME LIBRARY PRESS

FAIRBANKS, INDIANA

ALL RIGHTS RESERVED.

No part of this book may be reproduced or transmitted in any form or by any means, electronic or mechanical, including photocopying, recording, or by any information storage or retrieval system, without written permission from the publisher.

Thank you!

A Word about St. Jerome School

St. Jerome School is a branch of St. Jerome Library, the parent nonprofit organization to our mission of helping Catholic families to homeschool by providing affordable options in the most important vocation of raising saints for heaven. St. Jerome School & Library is a publisher, a true library, a bookstore, and a school, in the sense of providing teaching materials and lesson plans.

We use a simple, classic approach to education. Many of the items included in our lesson plans are from time-tested traditional sources. Some books, like our readers have been used in Catholic Schools since the early 1900s. Others are recent publications published with very sound, traditional Catholic doctrine and modest illustrations, all with no infections of modernism or other heresies. We are excited to share these wonderful books with you and your students. We truly hope that you will enjoy teaching with us!

Our school year is based on 36 weeks.

These items are for sale in our store, which you can find at www.stjeromelibrary.org

Books Highly Recommended for Family Daily/Weekly Use with our Curriculum

We highly recommend Catholic families say each day their morning prayers, evening prayers, Angelus (or Regina Caeli during Eastertide), and Family Rosary. Making Spiritual Communions is greatly encouraged during these difficult times of ours, and you can make frequent visits to the cemetery to pray for the Holy Souls in Purgatory.

In aiding the family with young children, we highly recommend these incredible books to boost the spiritual life:

Draw Us after Thee: Daily Indulgenced Devotions for Catholics which has a different daily prayer and picture for every day of the year to enchance morning prayers. Catholics reap the benefits of never being in danger of a stale prayer life while learning about the different feasts of the Church and incredible indulgences She offers to us. Indulgences can be given to the Holy Souls in Purgatory as well!

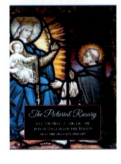

Pictorial Lives of the Saints, which has wonderful short stories & reflections of the saints' lives for daily meditation. Great for inspiring questions and "teaching moments". Stories are fairly short as to keep children's attention.

The Pictorial Rosary is a great aid for meditation during the Family Rosary, as well as including the excellent prayers to Our Lady of Sorrows which adds an excellent addition to family night prayers.

Feeding God's People

Providence Pastures Co. is a nonprofit formed by us, exclusively for advancing the Kingship of Christ and helping Our Lady and St. Joseph harbor and advance the family and domestic Church. We have come to see ourselves as stewards of creation and hope to share the undeniable goodness and health benefits of pasture-raised, nutrient-dense food. In these trying times, we see our work as an apostolate from Our Blessed Mother to feed Her children by providing affordable, healthy foods, such as organic grass-fed and finished, pasture-raised beef, chicken, pork, maple syrup, wheat products, produce, and more. Visit our certified organic farm's website at www.pasturesofprovidence.com Contact us through the website if you are interested in food being shipped to you. May God be with you!

Grade Four

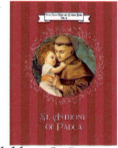

Art – This year the student will use the imaginative book, *Story Art Appreciation*. This adventurous new book begins with introducing art concepts. Then it launches into inspiring the student creatively with presenting great works of art which may inspire a story. The idea is to get the student to think originally and tell a story with the pictures. There are no correct answers here. Hopefully this will also be a good chance to get to know your student a little better. In this grade, we also ask that the child be given the choice of one of the twenty-four of the beautiful Mary Fabyan Windeatt coloring books available at St. Jerome Library's bookstore. This way the child can learn more about the saint of their choice and also get to work on their creative expression through coloring the lovely pictures.

Geography – *DK Geography: 4th Grade* extends your child's geographical knowledge and map-reading skills. This workbook includes a detailed look at each continent, physical features, and types of map, with a focus on different maps of the United States.

Grammar – This year continues the use of the old Catholic *Voyages in English* series from the 1950s with our updated and beautiful *St. Jerome Grammar* series. The *St. Jerome Grammar 4* text will give your child the foundation necessary for excellent grammar skills. *St. Jerome Grammar 4 Text Teacher's Manual* will give answers and instructions for teaching with the text. The *St. Jerome Grammar 4 Workbook* is filled with fun and edifying color pictures to drive home what your student has learned from the text. The *St. Jerome Grammar 4 Workbook Answer Key* will help immensely in speeding the process of grading with handy side-by-side answers to match the workbooks. A grammar notebook can be used for assigning writing assignments as needed.

Handwriting – We are excited to be using the newly reprinted *Catholic Penmanship Grade 4* book, a classic traditional Catholic handwriting series. These books are filled with edifying pictures and concepts of the Faith, as well as providing excellent practice for the beautiful skill of handwriting. The student will also need *Holy Family Writing Paper* with ½" lines for some of the exercises included in *Catholic Penmanship*. We sell these in our store, or you can buy them elsewhere.

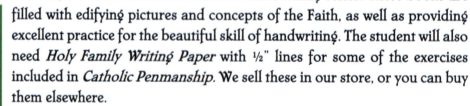

History – This year continues with the classical Catholic history series *Catholic Voyages in History* which has been used for decades with Catholic schools, even to present day. The *Old World Treasures* set for this year includes the textbook, workbook, and answer key. This lesson plan book includes the quarterly exams used as well for the course. The workbook will be used with the textbook in finding answers for weekly assignments. Quarterly exams should be given. the parent/teacher may decide if they allow the student open-book exams or not, depending on what he/she believes to be the best for their student(s). *Stories of Pioneer Life* is a fascinated storybook of true tales from the early pioneers of America. After reading about the sacrifices made by our ancestors, dangerous encounters with Native Americans and wild animals, the student will hopefully walk away with a much greater appreciation of how our country has come to be shaped.

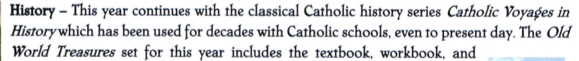

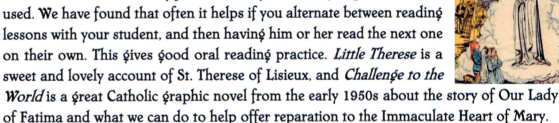
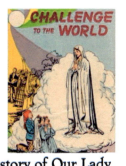

Reading – *St. Jerome School Reader 4* is an incredible, classic Catholic reader that has been used for over a hundred years with students! The historical content also helps children learn about times long past, including the beautiful speech that was used. We have found that often it helps if you alternate between reading lessons with your student, and then having him or her read the next one on their own. This gives good oral reading practice. *Little Therese* is a sweet and lovely account of St. Therese of Lisieux, and *Challenge to the World* is a great Catholic graphic novel from the early 1950s about the story of Our Lady of Fatima and what we can do to help offer reparation to the Immaculate Heart of Mary.

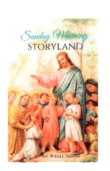

Religion – *Living for God, Book 4 Text* is from the 1940s' imprimatured *Living My Religion* series which teaches catechism in a fun and traditional way. The text is written in an easy-to-read format so that the child feels invited and excited to practice reading with the simple text. *Sunday Morning Storyland* is a simply lovely book that offers a short talk to children based on the liturgical year. It is best read every Sunday after the family gets home from Mass because it often addresses the Gospel of the Mass that day. It will not be mentioned in the lesson plans, but please do read it to all of your children on each Sunday.

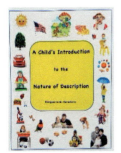

Logic – This year begins an incredible series which teaches the young Catholic an indispensable foundation of all definition and correct reasoning. The logic books are continued in grades 6 & 7 as well, building the child's ability to communicate ideas, thoughts, and understanding accurately. Before beginning classes, parents should read "A Child's Introduction to the Nature of Description" on p. iii-xv.

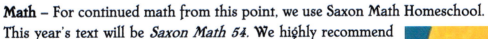

Math – For continued math from this point, we use Saxon Math Homeschool. This year's text will be *Saxon Math 54*. We highly recommend you also purchase *Saxon Math 54 Solutions Manual* to help with fast grading. If you trust your student, it may prove beneficial to have them grade their own math lessons after they have done them to learn what they have done wrong. Teachers, of course, grade tests so they can gauge what the student has been learning well. This works well especially in large, busy families where a mother is trying to grade many children's lessons each day. It can be overwhelming! *Saxon Math 54 Tests & Worksheets* should also be purchased as the tests are in it, as well as the activities and math drills. We will only be doing one of each math drill. Teachers may assign more if she sees there is a great need for the student to work more on a particular skill. For Mixed Practice, we suggest doing either odds or evens only.

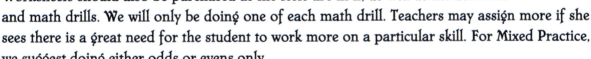
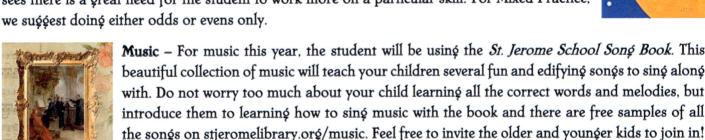

Music – For music this year, the student will be using the *St. Jerome School Song Book*. This beautiful collection of music will teach your children several fun and edifying songs to sing along with. Do not worry too much about your child learning all the correct words and melodies, but introduce them to learning how to sing music with the book and there are free samples of all the songs on stjeromelibrary.org/music. Feel free to invite the older and younger kids to join in!

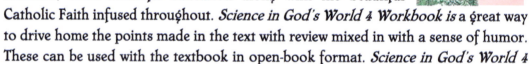

Science – is a classic and colorful science textbook which reflects the Catholic faith. It presents science in a simple, educational way with questions and basic facts, as well as providing opportunities to discuss the subjects with the teacher and offering optional experiments. We hope you will enjoy this series as we at St. Jerome Library Press have updated many of the pictures to include modern-day updates so that students will have excellent, solid scientific education along with the beautiful Catholic Faith infused throughout. *Science in God's World 4 Workbook* is a great way to drive home the points made in the text with review mixed in with a sense of humor. These can be used with the textbook in open-book format. *Science in God's World 4 Answer Key* is necessary for grading everything in this science course. *Weather and Other Natural Disasters*, is a Catholic educational activity book about weather and natural disasters which will help prepare your child for such events, as well as explain some of the majesty of God's creation in our world.

Spelling – This year's spelling continues with *Spelling Mountain Grade 4*. This speller is filled with beautiful mountain-themed pages, including many Catholic exercises, which make learning vocabulary, spelling, and a bit of handwriting practice one of our students' favorite activities. The words include Catholic terminology, along with words compiled from grade-appropriate standards used in national spelling bees and the like. If the teacher does not already own it, *St. Jerome Catholic Spellers Answer Key* will be essential for grading the "Fill in the Blank" and "Synonyms & Antonyms" sections of the workbook. A Spelling Notebook will be used to write the words for tests or as practice for those words that were done incorrectly on the pretest.

Summer Reading – For the summer, we would like to students to keep up their reading habits somewhat. The Summer Reading List for Grade 4 are the Windeatt books: *Saint Catherine of Siena, Saint Thomas Aquinas, The Miraculous Medal*, and *Patron Saint of First Communicants*. Having the child write a short book report on each describing characters, plot, and what they liked best is also a great idea. The book report is in the back of this book and may be copied for book report assignments, especially summer reading.

<u>Student will also need:</u>

Compass (for drawing circles)

Crayons

Folder

Pencils

Pens

Protractor

Ruler w/cm & in

Scissors

Grammar Notebook

Math Notebook

Spelling Notebook

In the lesson plan, * means refer to Comments section for the week

The Report Card is in the back for easy record keeping.

Sample

Spaces below the assignments are for grades, comments, time spent, etc.

	Kindergarten Lesson Plans		
Subject	Monday	Tuesday	Wednesday
Hand-writing & Phonics	-HK: Sing the ABC Song with student while on p. ix & count #'s, then p. xi-xiv	-HK: ABC Song with p. x, then p. 1-3 -ABC: Read p. 2-9	-HK: Review ABC's with student daily until understood, then p. 4-6 -ABC: Review p. 4-9
	N/A	95%	30min, 98%
Hand-writing & Phonics	-HK: p. 13-15 -ABC: p. 11-17	-HK: p. 16-18 -ABC: Review p. 11-17	-HK: p. 19-21 -ABC: Review p. 11-17
	100%, hard worker!	87%, rushed and distracted	92%

Book Abbreviations for Grade 4 Lesson Plans

Catholic Penmanship Grade 4 = CP4

Challenge to the World = CW

A Child's Introduction to the Nature of Description = CIND

DK Geography: 4th Grade = DKG4

Little Therese = LT

Living My Religion Grade 4 = LMR4

The Mountain of Mystery = MM

Old World Treasures Text = OWT

Old World Treasures Workbook = OWTWB

Saxon Math 54 Tests & Worksheets = SMTW4

Saxon Math 54 Text = SM4

Science in God's World 4 = SGW4

Science in God's World 4 Workbook = SGW4WB

Spelling Mountain Grade 4 = SM

St. Jerome Grammar 4 Text = SJG4

St. Jerome Grammar 4 Workbook = SJG4WB

St. Jerome School Reader 4 = SJSR4

St. Jerome School Song Book = SJSSB

Stories of Pioneer Life = SPL

Story Art Appreciation = SAA

Weather and Other Natural Disasters = WND

Windeatt Coloring Book of Student's Choice = WCB

Week 1

Subject	Monday	Tuesday	Wednesday
Religion			-LMR4: p. 1-13 (Teacher & student may alternatively read. Teacher orally asks test questions of the student for grade.)
Handwriting & Spelling	-CP4: p. 1 -SM: p. 3-6, Student reads words aloud to teacher for correct pronunciation, then writes words	-SM: p. 7-8	
Grammar	-SJG4: Read p. 2-11 (Stop at "Letters") It is recommended that teacher reads to student and then asks student to orally do some of*	-SJG4WB: p. 5	-SJG4WB: p. 6
Reading & Music		-SJSR4: p. 17-25 It is recommended to take turns reading aloud with the student. This gives the student practice with*	-SJSR4: p. 26-33
History & Logic	-CIND: Discuss and introduce p. xiv-xv	-OWTWB: p. 1-2	-CIND: Introduce and discuss p. 1-17
Math	-SM4: L. 1, student reads lessons to himself, then does Lesson Practice, and evens (or odds) only Mixed Practice in MN	-SM4: L. 2 -SMTW4: Facts Practice Test A (these may be done more than once if teacher wishes)	-SM4: L. 3
Science	Parent look at WND p. 82 to see if you would like to do the experiment and get the supplies ready at the right time.	-SGW4: Student read p. 5-10 -SGW4WB: p. 3	-SGW4: Read p. 11-12 -SGW4WB: p. 4
Art & Geography	-DKG4: p. 4-5	-WCB: Ch. 1 Read & Color	

Week 1

Subject	Thursday	Friday	Comments
Religion			*Don't forget to read Sunday Morning Storyland on each Sunday after Mass until the book is complete.
Hand-writing & Spelling	-SM: Administer pre-test. Student writes words in Spelling notebook 3x each that are wrong.	-CP4: p. 2 -SM: Take Post-test for grade.	
Grammar	-SJG4WB: p. 7		*the exercises in the book to gauge understanding. Workbooks assignments will be done on their own.
Reading & Music		-SJSSB: Practice Gr. 4 songs #1-2, p. 23-24. Song files are on stjeromelibrary.org/music. Feel free to sing more songs of interest.	*public speaking, as well as listening to how it should be read.
History & Logic	-OWT: read p. 1-6 -OWTWB: p. 3	-SPL: Read "To the Children" and p. 1-12*	*This can be read alone by the student.
Math	-SM4: L. 4 -SMTW4: Activity Sheets 1-6	-SM4: L. 5	
Science		-WND: Read through p. 2-8. Student will write the dates on the September calendar (or the month you are in) and start recording*	*the weather for each day. Use simplified forms of the symbols on p. 7. Write dates on the calendar as you begin each month.
Art & Geo-graphy	-SAA: Teacher read p. 2 before beginning. Teacher read and talk about p. 3-5 with student.		

Week 2

Subject	Monday	Tuesday	Wednesday
Religion			-LMR4: p. 14-25
Handwriting & Spelling	-CP4: p. 3 -SM: p. 9-12, Lesson 2	-SM: p. 13-14	
Grammar	-SJG4: p. 8-22 Stop at "Teamwork" (Explain how our zip codes have changed since the 1950s.)*	-SJG4WB: p. 8-9	-SJG4WB: p. 10
Reading & Music		-SJSR4: p. 34-43	-SJSR4: p. 44-52
History & Logic	-CIND: p. 76-79	-OWT: read p. 9-15 -OWTWB: p. 4-5	-CIND: p. 80-81
Math	-SM4: L. 6	-SM4: L. 7	-SM4: L. 8 -SMTW: FPT B
Science	WND: Don't forget to record the weather.	-SGW4: read p. 13-14 -SGW4WB: p. 5 -WND: Record the weather.	-SGW4: read p. 15-17 -SGW4WB: p. 6 -WND: Record the weather.
Art & Geography	-DKG4: p. 6-7	-WCB: Ch. 2 Read & Color	

Week 2

Subject	Thursday	Friday	Comments
Religion			
Hand-writing & Spelling	-SM: Administer pre-test. Student writes words in Spelling notebook 3x each that are wrong.	-CP4: p. 4 (on pages such as these without much room, the student* -SM: Take Post-test for grade.	*will trace and then write the exercise on their writing paper
Grammar			*Teacher will assign writing assignments from SJG4 according to the student's needs to write in his Grammar notebook.
Reading & Music		-SJSSB: Practice Gr. 4 songs #1-2, p. 23-24. Song files are on stjeromelibrary.org/music. Feel free to sing more songs of interest.	
History & Logic	-OWT: read p. 15-25	-SPL: Read p. 13-20	
Math	-SM4: L. 9	-SM4: L. 10	
Science	-WND: Record the weather.	-WND: Record the weather. Do p. 18.	
Art & Geography	-SAA: teacher read p. 6-7 with student and discuss		

Subject	Monday	Tuesday	Wednesday
Religion			-LMR4: p. 26-34
Hand-writing & Spelling	-CP4: p. 5 -SM: p. 15-18, L. 3	-SM: p. 19-20	
Grammar	-SJG4: p. 22-33 (Stop at "Opposites")	-SJG4WB: p. 11	-SJG4WB: p. 12
Reading & Music		-SJSR4: p. 53-61	-SJSR4: p. 62-71
History & Logic	-CIND: Game p. 20-21	-OWTWB: p. 6-7	-CIND: Quiz p. 18-19
Math	-SMTW4: Test 1	-SM4: Investigation 1	-SM4: L. 11
Science	-WND: Continue to record the weather for each day throughout the month of May.	-SGW4: read p. 18-19 -SGW4WB: p. 7	-SGW4: read p. 20-21 -SGW4WB: p. 8
Art & Geography	-DKG4: p. 8-9	-WCB: Ch. 3 Read & Color	

Week 3

Subject	Thursday	Friday	Comments
Religion			
Hand-writing & Spelling	-SM: Administer pre-test. Student writes words in Spelling notebook 3x each that are wrong.	-CP4: p. 6 -SM: Take Post-test for grade.	
Grammar	-SJG4WB: p. 13		
Reading & Music		-SJSSB: Practice Gr. 4 songs #1-2, p. 23-24. Song files are on stjeromelibrary.org/music. Feel free to sing more songs of interest.	
History & Logic	-OWT: read p. 28-32 -OWTWB: p. 8	-SPL: Read p. 21-28	
Math	-SM4: L. 12 -SMTW4: Activity Sheet 7	-SM4: L. 13	
Science		-WND: Do p. 19	
Art & Geography	-SAA: teacher read p. 8-10 with student and discuss		

Week 4

Subject	Monday	Tuesday	Wednesday
Religion			-LMR4: p. 35-45
Hand-writing & Spelling	-CP4: p. 7 -SM: p. 21-24, L. 4	-SM: p. 25-26	
Grammar	-SJG4: p. 33-39 (Stop at "Contractions")	-SJG4WB: p. 14	-SJG4WB: p. 15
Reading & Music		-SJSR4: p. 72-80	-SJSR4: p. 81-89
History & Logic	-CIND: Introduce & discuss p. 22-39	-OWT: read p. 32-38	-CIND: Review p. 22-39
Math	-SM4: L. 14 -SMTW4: Activity Sheet 8	-SM4: L. 15	-SMTW4: Test 2
Science		-SGW4: read p. 22-23 -SGW4WB: p. 9	-SGW4: read p. 24 -SGW4WB: p. 10
Art & Geography	-DKG4: p. 10-11	-WCB: Ch. 4 Read & Color	

Subject	Thursday	Friday	Comments
Religion			
Hand-writing & Spelling	-SM: Administer pre-test. Student writes words in Spelling notebook 3x each that are wrong.	-CP4: p. 8 -SM: Take Post-test for grade.	
Grammar	-SJG4WB: p. 16-17		
Reading & Music		-SJSSB: Practice Gr. 4 songs #1-2, p. 23-24. Song files are on stjeromelibrary.org/music. Feel free to sing more songs of interest.	
History & Logic	-OWTWB: p. 9-10	-SPL: Read p. 29-32	
Math	-SM4: L. 16 -SMTW4: Activity Sheet 9	-SM4: L. 17	
Science		-WND: Do p. 20	
Art & Geography	-SAA: teacher read p. 11-13 with student and discuss		

Week 4

Week 5

Subject	Monday	Tuesday	Wednesday
Religion			-LMR4: p. 46-52
Hand-writing & Spelling	-CP4: p. 9 -SM: p. 27-30, L. 5	-SM: p. 31-32	
Grammar	-SJG4: p. 39-51	-SJG4WB: p. 18	-SJG4WB: p. 19
Reading & Music		-SJSR4: p. 90-99	-SJSR4: p. 100-107
History & Logic	-CIND: p. 82-87	-OWT: read p. 41-48 -OWTWB: p. 11	-CIND: p. 88-89
Math	-SM4: L. 18 -SMTW4: Activity Sheet 10	-SM4: L. 19	-SM4: L. 20
Science	-WND: Keep recording the weather each day. 😊	-SGW4: read p. 25-27 -SGW4WB: p. 11	-SGW4: read p. 28 -SGW4WB: p. 12
Art & Geography	-DKG4: p. 12-13	-WCB: Ch. 5 Read & Color	

		Week 5	
Subject	Thursday	Friday	Comments
Religion			
Hand-writing & Spelling	-SM: Administer pre-test. Student writes words in Spelling notebook 3x each that are wrong.	-CP4: p. 10 -SM: Take Post-test for grade.	
Grammar	-SJG4WB: p. 20		
Reading & Music		-SJSSB: Practice Gr. 4 songs #3-4, p. 25-27. Song files are on stjeromelibrary.org/music. Feel free to sing more songs of interest.	
History & Logic	-OWT: read p. 48-54 -OWTWB: p. 12-13	-SPL: Read p. 33-45	
Math	-SMTW4: Test 3	-SM4: Investigation 2	
Science		-WND: Read p. 21-26	
Art & Geography	-SAA: teacher read p. 14-15 with student and discuss		

Week 6

Subject	Monday	Tuesday	Wednesday
Religion			-LMR4: p. 53-64
Hand-writing & Spelling	-CP4: p. 11 -SM: p. 33-36, L. 6	-SM: p. 37-38	
Grammar	-SJG4: p. 52-66	-SJG4WB: p. 21	-SJG4WB: p. 22-23
Reading & Music		-SJSR4: p. 108-114	-SJSR4: p. 115-126
History & Logic	-CIND: Game p. 42-43	-OWT: read p. 54-64	-CIND: Quiz p. 40-41
Math	-SM4: L. 21 -SMTW4: Activity Sheet 12	-SM4: L. 22	-SM4: L. 23 -SMTW4: Activity Sheet 13
Science	-WND: Continue to record the weather each day until the end of the school year.	-SGW4: read p. 29-31 -SGW4WB: p. 13	-SGW4: read p. 32-33 -SGW4WB: p. 14
Art & Geography	-DKG4: p. 14-15	-WCB: Ch. 6 Read & Color	

Week 6

Subject	Thursday	Friday	Comments
Religion			
Hand-writing & Spelling	-SM: Administer pre-test. Student writes words in Spelling notebook 3x each that are wrong.	-CP4: p. 12 -SM: Take Post-test for grade.	
Grammar	-SJG4WB: p. 24		
Reading & Music		-SJSSB: Practice Gr. 4 songs #3-4, p. 25-27. Song files are on stjeromelibrary.org/music. Feel free to sing more songs of interest.	
History & Logic	-OWTWB: p. 14-15	-SPL: Read p. 46-53	
Math	-SM4: L. 24	-SM4: L. 25	
Science		-WND: Read p. 27-28. Do p. 29.	
Art & Geography	-SAA: teacher read p. 16-17 with student and discuss		

Week 7

Subject	Monday	Tuesday	Wednesday
Religion			-LMR4: p. 65-73
Hand-writing & Spelling	-CP4: p. 49 Unit practice -SM: p. 39-42, L. 7	-SM: p. 43-44	
Grammar	-SJG4: p. 67-71 (Stop at "No Words")	-SJG4WB: p. 25	-SJG4WB: p. 26
Reading & Music		-SJSR4: p. 127-135	-SJSR4: p. 136-143
History & Logic	-CIND: Introduce & discuss p. 44-53	-OWT: read p. 67-75 -OWTWB: p. 16-17	-CIND: p. 90-93
Math	-SMTW4: Test 4	-SM4: L. 26	-SM4: L. 27
Science		-SGW4: read p. 34-36, do questions on p. 36 orally with teacher -SGW4WB: p. 15	-SGW4: read p. 37-39 -SGW4WB: p. 16
Art & Geo-graphy	-DKG4: p. 16-17	-WCB: Ch. 7 Read & Color	

Week 7

Subject	Thursday	Friday	Comments
Religion			
Hand-writing & Spelling	-SM: Administer pre-test. Student writes words in Spelling notebook 3x each that are wrong.	-CP4: p. 13 -SM: Take Post-test for grade.	
Grammar	-SJG4WB: p. 27		
Reading & Music		-SJSSB: Practice Gr. 4 songs #3-4, p. 25-27. Song files are on stjeromelibrary.org/music. Feel free to sing more songs of interest.	
History & Logic	-OWT: read p. 75-84 -OWTWB: p. 18-19	-SPL: Read p. 54-68	
Math	-SM4: L. 28	-SM4: L. 29 -SMTW4: FPT C	
Science		-WND: Read p. 30-34	
Art & Geo-graphy	-SAA: teacher read p. 18-19 with student and discuss		

Week 8

Subject	Monday	Tuesday	Wednesday
Religion			-LMR4: p. 74-86
Hand-writing & Spelling	-CP4: p. 14 -SM: p. 45-48, L. 8	-SM: p. 49-50	
Grammar	-SJG4: p. 71-74	-SJG4WB: p. 28	-SJG4WB: p. 29
Reading & Music		-SJSR4: p. 144-152	-SJSR4: p. 153-160
History & Logic	-CIND: Game p. 56-57	-OWTWB: p. 20-21 (Review A-C)	-CIND: Quiz p. 54-55
Math	-SM4: L. 30	-SMTW4: Test 5	-SM4: Investigation 3 -SMTW4: Activity Sheets 14-15
Science		-SGW4: read p. 40-43 -SGW4WB: p. 17	-SGW4: read p. 44-47 -SGW4WB: p. 18
Art & Geography	-DKG4: p. 18	-WCB: Ch. 8 Read & Color	

Week 8

Subject	Thursday	Friday	Comments
Religion			
Hand-writing & Spelling	-SM: Administer pre-test. Student writes words in Spelling notebook 3x each that are wrong.	-CP4: p. 15 -SM: Take Post-test for grade.	
Grammar	-SJG4WB: p. 30		
Reading & Music		-SJSSB: Practice Gr. 4 songs #3-4, p. 25-27. Song files are on stjeromelibrary.org/music. Feel free to sing more songs of interest.	
History & Logic	-OWTWB: p. 21-22 (Review D-E)	-SPL: Read p. 69-78	
Math	-SM4: L. 31	-SM4: L. 32	
Science		-WND: Read p. 35. Do p. 36.	
Art & Geo-graphy	-SAA: teacher read p. 20-21 with student and discuss		

Subject	Monday	Tuesday	Wednesday
Religion			-LMR4: p. 87-97
Hand-writing & Spelling	-CP4: p. 16		
Grammar	-SJG4: p. 75-80 (Stop at "Contractions")	-SJG4WB: p. 31	-SJG4WB: p. 32
Reading & Music		-SJSR4: p. 161-168	-SJSR4: p. 169-179
History & Logic	-CIND: Introduce & discuss p. 58-69	-OWTWB: p. 23-24 (Review F-H) Study for First Quarter Exam	-OWT: Study for First Quarter Exam -CIND: Review p. 58-69
Math	-SM4: L. 33 -SMTW4: Activity Sheet 16	-SM4: L. 34 -SMTW4: Activity Sheet 17	-SM4: L. 35
Science		-SGW4: read p. 48-51 -SGW4WB: p. 19	-SGW4: read p. 52-55 -SGW4WB: p. 20
Art & Geography	-DKG4: p. 19	-WCB: Ch. 9 Read & Color	

Week 9

Subject	Thursday	Friday	Comments
Religion			
Hand-writing & Spelling		-CP4: p. 17	
Grammar	-SJG4WB: p. 33		
Reading & Music		-SJSSB: Practice Gr. 4 songs #5-6, p. 28-29. Song files are on stjeromelibrary.org/music. Feel free to sing more songs of interest.	
History & Logic	**-First Quarter Exam** (remove exam two pages from here)	-SPL: Read p. 79-90	
Math	-SMTW4: Test 6		
Science		-WND: Do p. 37	
Art & Geography			

First Quarter History Exam

Old World Treasures

Grade 4

Name _____

Fill in the Blanks (some will not be used):

Babylonians	"Black Land"	fire	Nile
Rosetta	David	History	astronomers
365	government	300	Tiber

1. _____ is the name given to the study of things which happened a very long time ago.

2. The first important discovery made by early man was the use of _____.

3. Men need some form of _____ so that they can live in an orderly way and keep peace with one another.

4. The _____ River flows through Egypt.

5. In the Egyptian calendar there were _____ days in the year.

6. The key to Egyptian writing was the _____ stone.

7. The Egyptians called their land _____.

8. People who study the heavens are called _____.

9. Hammurabi was the king of the _____.

10. The Book of Psalms were written by King _____.

In front of each of the items in Column B, write the number of the word or phrase in Column A which is most closely connected with it.

Column A	Column B
1. writing of the ancient Babylonians	( ) stylus
2. a fine wood for ships	( ) Alexander the Great
3. the pencil of the Babylonians	( ) Hellenistic
4. son of Philip	( ) simple
5. "Father of History"	( ) Demosthenes
6. Alexander built up a new culture called	( ) cedar
7. Greece is a	( ) Europe
8. life in ancient Athens was	( ) peninsula
9. a great Greek orator	( ) Herodotus
10. Greece is in the continent of	( ) cuneiform writing

Circle yes if the statement is correct. Circle no if it is not correct.

yes **no**   1. The Alps mountains separate Italy from the rest of Europe.

yes **no**   2. Rome was first ruled by pharaohs.

yes **no**   3. The Circus Maximus was the place where chariot races were held.

yes **no**   4. The Egyptian statue which has the body of a lion and a human head is called a sphinx.

yes **no**   5. The Spartan children were fearless.

yes **no**   6. Brutus was an unwise, cruel traitor.

yes **no**   7. The city of Rome is in Greece.

yes **no**   8. Julius Caesar was an ambitious ruler who wanted to govern Greece.

yes **no**   9. France used to be called Gaul.

yes **no**   10. The central point in all history is the Birth of Christ.

Week 10

Subject	Monday	Tuesday	Wednesday
Religion			-LMR4: p. 98-107
Hand-writing & Spelling	-CP4: p. 18 -SM: p. 51-54, L. 9	SM: p. 55-56	
Grammar	-SJG4: p. 80-86	-SJG4WB: p. 34	-SJG4WB: p. 35
Reading & Music		-SJSR4: p. 180-190	-SJSR4: p. 191-199
History & Logic	-CIND: p. 94-97	-OWT: read p. 87-98	-CIND: p. 98-99
Math	-SM4: L. 36	-SM4: L. 37 -SMTW4: FPT D	-SM4: L. 38 -SMTW4: FPT E, Activity Sheet 18
Science		-SGW4: read p. 56 -SGW4WB: p. 21	-SGW4: read p. 57-58 -SGW4WB: p. 22
Art & Geo-graphy	-DKG4: p. 20	-WCB: Ch. 10 Read & Color	

Week 10

Subject	Thursday	Friday	Comments
Religion			
Hand-writing & Spelling	-SM: Administer pre-test. Student writes words in Spelling notebook 3x each that are wrong.	-CP4: p. 19 -SM: Take Post-test for grade.	
Grammar	-SJG4WB: p. 36		
Reading & Music		-SJSSB: Practice Gr. 4 songs #5-6, p. 28-29. Song files are on stjeromelibrary.org/music. Feel free to sing more songs of interest.	
History & Logic	-OWTWB: p. 25-26	-SPL: Read p. 91-102	
Math	-SM4: L. 39 -SMTW4: FPT F	-SM4: L. 40	
Science		-WND: Do p. 38. Answer key is in the back. Student may correct their own work if he is trustworthy.	
Art & Geography	-SAA: teacher read p. 22-23 with student and discuss		

Week 11

Subject	Monday	Tuesday	Wednesday
Religion			-LMR4: p. 108-120
Hand-writing & Spelling	-CP4: p. 20 -SM: p. 57-60, L. 10	-SM: p. 61-62	
Grammar	-SJG4: p. 87-104	-SJG4WB: p. 37	-SJG4WB: p. 38
Reading & Music		-SJSR4: p. 200-209	-SJSR4: p. 210-217
History & Logic	-CIND: p. 100-103	-OWT: read p. 102-109	-CIND: Game p. 72-73 Quiz p. 70-71
Math	-SMTW4: Test 7	-SM4: Investigation 4: #1-30	-SM4: Investigation 4 #31-70 evens
Science		-SGW4: read p. 59-60 -SGW4WB: p. 23	-SGW4: read p. 61-62 -SGW4WB: p. 24
Art & Geography	-DKG4: p. 21	-WCB: Ch. 11 Read & Color	

Week 11

Subject	Thursday	Friday	Comments
Religion			
Hand-writing & Spelling	-SM: Administer pre-test. Student writes words in Spelling notebook 3x each that are wrong.	-CP4: p. 21 -SM: Take Post-test for grade.	
Grammar	-SJG4WB: p. 39		
Reading & Music		-SJSSB: Practice Gr. 4 songs #5-6, p. 28-29. Song files are on stjeromelibrary.org/music. Feel free to sing more songs of interest.	
History & Logic	-OWTWB: p. 27-28	-SPL: Read p. 103-116	
Math	-SM4: L. 41	-SM4: L. 42	
Science		-WND: Read p. 39	
Art & Geography	-SAA: teacher read p. 24-25 with student and discuss		

Week 12

Subject	Monday	Tuesday	Wednesday
Religion			-LMR4: p. 121-129
Hand-writing & Spelling	-CP4: p. 22 -SM: p. 63-66, L. 11	-SM: p. 67-68	
Grammar	-SJG4: p. 105-108 (Stop at "Opposites")	-SJG4WB: p. 40	-SJG4WB: p. 41
Reading & Music		-SJSR4: p. 218-226	-SJSR4: p. 227-235
History & Logic	-CIND: Review p. 1-17 and 22-39	-OWT: read p. 109-112	-CIND: Review p. 44-53
Math	-SM4: L. 43	-SM4: L. 44	-SM4: L. 45
Science		-SGW4: read p. 63-64 -SGW4WB: p. 25	-SGW4: read p. 65-67 -SGW4WB: p. 26
Art & Geography	-DKG4: p. 22	-WCB: Ch. 12 Read & Color	

Week 12

Subject	Thursday	Friday	Comments
Religion			
Hand-writing & Spelling	-SM: Administer pre-test. Student writes words in Spelling notebook 3x each that are wrong.	-CP4: p. 23 -SM: Take Post-test for grade.	
Grammar	-SJG4WB: p. 42		
Reading & Music		-SJSSB: Practice Gr. 4 songs #5-6, p. 28-29. Song files are on stjeromelibrary.org/music. Feel free to sing more songs of interest.	
History & Logic	-OWTWB: p. 29-30	-SPL: Read p. 117-136 (end!) -Ask the child what they learned. Did they enjoy the book?	
Math	-SMTW4: Test 8	-SM4: L. 46	
Science		-WND: Do p. 40	
Art & Geography	-SAA: teacher read p. 26-27 with student and discuss		

Week 13

Subject	Monday	Tuesday	Wednesday
Religion			-LMR4: p. 130-137
Hand-writing & Spelling	-CP4: p. 49, Unit practice -SM: p. 69-72, L. 12	-SM: p. 73-74	
Grammar	-SJG4: p. 108-112 (Stop at "The Comma in Direct Quotations")	-SJG4WB: p. 43	-SJG4WB: p. 44
Reading & Music		-SJSR4: p. 236-242	-SJSR4: p. 243-251
History & Logic	-CIND: Review p. 58-69	-OWT: read p. 115-122	-CIND: p. 74-75 and 104-107
Math	-SM4: L. 47	-SM4: L. 48	-SM4: L. 49 -SMTW4: FPT G
Science		-SGW4: read p. 68-70 -SGW4WB: p. 27	-SGW4: read p. 71-74 Do questions on p. 74 orally with teacher -SGW4WB: p. 28
Art & Geography	-DKG4: p. 23	-WCB: Ch. 13 Read & Color	

Week 13

Subject	Thursday	Friday	Comments
Religion			
Hand-writing & Spelling	-SM: Administer pre-test. Student writes words in Spelling notebook 3x each that are wrong.	-CP4: p. 24 -SM: Take Post-test for grade.	
Grammar	-SJG4WB: p. 45		
Reading & Music		-SJSSB: Practice Gr. 4 songs #7-8, p. 30-31. Song files are on stjeromelibrary.org/music. Feel free to sing more songs of interest.	
History & Logic	-OWTWB: p. 31-33		
Math	-SM4: L. 50	-SMTW4: Test 9	
Science		-WND: Do p. 41.	
Art & Geography	-SAA: teacher read p. 28-29 with student and discuss		

Week 14

Subject	Monday	Tuesday	Wednesday
Religion			-LMR4: p. 138-154
Hand-writing & Spelling	-CP4: p. 25 -SM: p. 75-78, L. 13	-SM: p. 79-80	
Grammar	-SJG4: p. 112-118	-SJG4WB: p. 46	-SJG4WB: p. 47
Reading & Music		-SJSR4: p. 252-259	-SJSR4: p. 260-267
History & Logic	-CIND: p. 108-111	-OWT: read p. 122-126	-CIND: p. 112-115
Math	-SM4: Investigation 5 -SMTW4: Activity Sheet 22	-SM4: L. 51 -SMTW4: FPT H	-SM4: L. 52
Science		-SGW4: read p. 75-77 -SGW4WB: p. 29	-SGW4: read p. 78-79 -SGW4WB: p. 30
Art & Geography	-DKG4: p. 24	-WCB: Ch. 14 Read & Color	

Week 14

Subject	Thursday	Friday	Comments
Religion			
Hand-writing & Spelling	-SM: Administer pre-test. Student writes words in Spelling notebook 3x each that are wrong.	-CP4: p. 26 -SM: Take Post-test for grade.	
Grammar	-SJG4WB: p. 48		
Reading & Music		-SJSSB: Practice Gr. 4 songs #7-8, p. 30-31. Song files are on stjeromelibrary.org/music. Feel free to sing more songs of interest.	
History & Logic	-OWTWB: p. 34-35		
Math	-SM4: L. 53 -SMTW4: FPT I	-SM4: L. 54	
Science		-WND: Read p. 42. Do p. 43	
Art & Geography	-SAA: teacher read p. 30-31 with student and discuss		

Week 15

Subject	Monday	Tuesday	Wednesday
Religion			-LMR4: p. 155-172
Hand-writing & Spelling	-CP4: p. 27 -SM: p. 81-84, L. 14	-SM: p. 85-86	
Grammar	-SJG4: p. 119-132 (Stop at "Writing about Winter")	-SJG4WB: p. 49	-SJG4WB: p. 50-51
Reading & Music		-SJSR4: p. 268-277	-SJSR4: p. 278-286
History & Logic	-CIND: p. 116-119	-OWTWB: p. 36-37 (Review A-C)	-CIND: p. 120-121
Math	-SM4: L. 55	-SMTW4: Test 10	-SM4: L. 56
Science		-SGW4: read p. 80-81 -SGW4WB: p. 31	-SGW4: read p. 82-84 -SGW4WB: p. 32
Art & Geography	-DKG4: p. 25	-WCB: Ch. 15 Read & Color	

Week 15

Subject	Thursday	Friday	Comments
Religion			
Hand-writing & Spelling	-SM: Administer pre-test. Student writes words in Spelling notebook 3x each that are wrong.	-CP4: p. 28 -SM: Take Post-test for grade.	
Grammar	-SJG4WB: p. 52		
Reading & Music		-SJSSB: Practice Gr. 4 songs #7-8, p. 30-31. Song files are on stjeromelibrary.org/music. Feel free to sing more songs of interest.	
History & Logic	-OWTWB: p. 37-38 (Review D-E)		
Math	-SM4: L. 57 -SMTW: FPT J	-SM4: L. 58	
Science		-WND: Read p. 44-45. Do p. 46-47.	
Art & Geography	-SAA: teacher read p. 32-33 with student and discuss		

Week 16

Subject	Monday	Tuesday	Wednesday
Religion			-LMR4: p. 173-185 (Stop at "The Eighth Commandment")
Hand-writing & Spelling	-CP4: p. 29 -SM: p. 87-90, L. 15	-SM: p. 91-92	
Grammar	-SJG4: p. 132-142 (Stop at "Begin, Began, and Begun")	-SJG4WB: p. 53	-SJG4WB: p. 54
Reading & Music		-SJSR4: p. 287-297	-SJSR4: p. 298-306
History & Logic	-CIND: Introduce p. 122 and do p. 124-125	-OWT: read p. 128-133	-CIND: p. 126-127
Math	-SM4: L. 59	-SM4: L. 60	-SMTW4: Test 11
Science		-SGW4: read p. 85-86 -SGW4WB: p. 33-34	-SGW4: read p. 87-91 -SGW4WB: p. 35-36
Art & Geography	-DKG4: p. 26	-WCB: Ch. 16 Read & Color (end!)	

Week 16

Subject	Thursday	Friday	Comments
Religion			
Handwriting & Spelling	-SM: Administer pre-test. Student writes words in Spelling notebook 3x each that are wrong.	-CP4: p. 30 -SM: Take Post-test for grade.	
Grammar	-SJG4WB: p. 55		
Reading & Music		-SJSSB: Practice Gr. 4 songs #7-8, p. 30-31. Song files are on stjeromelibrary.org/music. Feel free to sing more songs of interest.	
History & Logic	-OWTWB: p. 39-40		
Math	-SM4: Investigation 6 -SMTW4: Activity Sheets 23-24	-SM4: L. 61	
Science		-WND: p. 48-51	
Art & Geography	-SAA: teacher read p. 34-35 with student and discuss		

Week 17

Subject	Monday	Tuesday	Wednesday
Religion			-LMR4: p. 185-195
Hand-writing & Spelling	-CP4: p. 31 -SM: p. 93-96, L. 16	-SM: p. 97-98	
Grammar	-SJG4: p. 142-145 (Stop at "Homonyms")	-SJG4WB: p. 56	-SJG4WB: p. 57
Reading & Music		-SJSR4: p. 307-316	-SJSR4: p. 317-326
History & Logic	-CIND: Introduce p. 123 and do p. 128-129	-OWT: read p. 133-138	-CIND: p. 130-131
Math	-SM4: L. 62	-SM4: L. 63	-SM4: L. 64
Science		-SGW4: read p. 92-95 -SGW4WB: p. 37	-SGW4: read p. 96-98 -SGW4WB: p. 38
Art & Geography	-DKG4: p. 27		

Week 17

Subject	Thursday	Friday	Comments
Religion			
Hand-writing & Spelling	-SM: Administer pre-test. Student writes words in Spelling notebook 3x each that are wrong.	-CP4: p. 32 -SM: Take Post-test for grade.	
Grammar	-SJG4WB: p. 58		
Reading & Music		-SJSSB: Practice Gr. 4 songs #9-10, p. 32-33. Song files are on stjeromelibrary.org/music. Feel free to sing more songs of interest.	
History & Logic	-OWTWB: p. 41-42		
Math	-SM4: L. 65	-SMTW4: Test 12	
Science		-WND: p. 52-54	
Art & Geography	-SAA: teacher read p. 36-37 with student and discuss		

Week 18

Subject	Monday	Tuesday	Wednesday
Religion			-LMR4: p. 196-208
Hand-writing & Spelling	-CP4: p. 33		
Grammar	-SJG4: p. 145-148	-SJG4WB: p. 59	-SJG4WB: p. 60
Reading & Music		-SJSR4: p. 327-335	-SJSR4: p. 336-342
History & Logic	-CIND: p. 132-133	-OWT: Study for Second Quarter Exam (covering p. 87-138)	-CIND: p. 134-136 (end!)
Math	-SM4: L. 66	-SM4: L. 67	-SM4: L. 68
Science		-SGW4: read p. 99-104 Do questions on p. 104 orally with teacher -SGW4WB: p. 39-41	-SGW4: read p. 105-109 -SGW4WB: p. 42
Art & Geography	-DKG4: p. 28		

Week 18

Subject	Thursday	Friday	Comments
Religion			
Hand-writing & Spelling		-CP4: p. 34	
Grammar	-SJG4WB: p. 61		
Reading & Music		-SJSSB: Practice Gr. 4 songs #9-10, p. 32-33. Song files are on stjeromelibrary.org/music. Feel free to sing more songs of interest.	
History & Logic	-Second Quarter Exam Remove exam two pages from here.		
Math			
Science		-WND: p. 55-56	
Art & Geography			

Second Quarter History Exam

Old World Treasures

Grade 4

Name _____

Fill in the Blanks (some will not be used):

St. Paul	St. Giles	Mary Magdalen	Olives
Christ	3	St. Peter	St. Joseph
Lazarus	Commandments	5	Pentecost

1. _____ came into the world as a tiny little baby, born in a cave in Bethlehem.

2. When Jesus was 12-years-old, He went to Jerusalem with Our Lady and _____.

3. St. Joseph and Our Lady were sorrowfully searching for Jesus in Jerusalem for _____ days.

4. Jesus raised his friend _____ from the dead because He felt sorry for his sisters, Martha and Mary.

5. After the Last Supper, Our Lord went to the Garden of _____.

6. Our Lord said at one time, "If you love Me, keep My _____."

7. After Jesus had risen from the tomb, He showed Himself first to _____.

8. Our Lord chose one of His Apostles, _____, to be the Head of His Church.

9. The Apostles received strength and power from the Holy Ghost on _____.

10. _____ is called the "Apostles of the Gentiles".

In front of each of the items in Column B, write the number of the word or phrase in Column A which is most closely connected with it.

Column A	Column B
1. Theodosius was taught by	( ) Diocletian
2. this man ordered the Scriptures to be burned	( ) Constantine
3. burial places of early Christians	( ) Cicero
4. converted while on his way to persecute Christians	( ) Justinian
5. first persecution of the Christians	( ) Huns
6. language of the ancient Romans	( ) catacombs
7. the greatest Roman orator	( ) Latin
8. "Body of the Civil Law"	( ) St. Paul
9. barbarians from central Asia	( ) Nero
10. Edict of Milan	( ) St. Ambrose

Circle yes if the statement is correct. Circle no if it is not correct.

yes   no   1. We should be very grateful to the Huns for the rapid spread of Christianity.

yes   no   2. Cicero and Pliny were masters in the art of letter writing.

yes   no   3. Canon Law is the law of the Greeks.

yes   no   4. "The blood of martyrs is the seed of the Church."

yes   no   5. For about 500 years after the Birth of Christ, the Roman Empire was at peace and the Romans enjoyed a great deal of comfort.

yes   no   6. The Romans were great builders and engineers.

yes   no   7. The Huns were wild nomads.

yes   no   8. Attila was the great leader of the Visigoths.

yes   no   9. The first king of the Franks was Clovis, who married Clotilde, a Catholic.

yes   no   10. Clovis and his followers were baptized by St. Remigius (Remi) who was the Bishop of Reims.

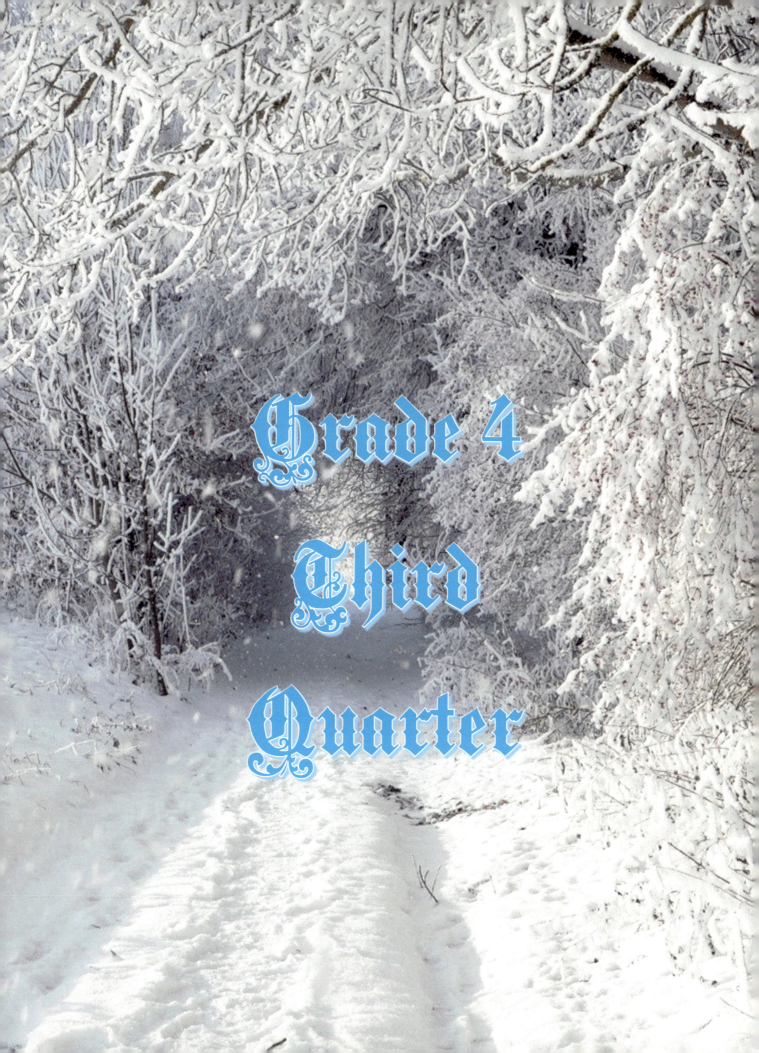

		Week 19	
Subject	Monday	Tuesday	Wednesday
Religion			-LMR4: p. 209-219
Hand-writing & Spelling	-CP4: p. 49, Unit practice -SM: p. 99-102, L. 17	-SM: p. 103-104	
Grammar	-SJG4: p. 149-167 (Stop at "Adding Picture Words")	-SJG4WB: p. 62	-SJG4WB: p. 63
Reading & Music		-SJSR4: p. 343-350	-SJSR4: p. 351-357
History & Logic		-OWT: read p. 141-144 -OWTWB: p. 43	
Math	-SM4: L. 69	-SM4: L. 70	-SMTW4: Test 13
Science		-SGW4: read p. 110-114 -SGW4WB: p. 43	-SGW4: read p. 115-117 -SGW4WB: p. 44
Art & Geography	-DKG4: p. 29		

Week 19

Subject	Thursday	Friday	Comments
Religion			
Hand-writing & Spelling	-SM: Administer pre-test. Student writes words in Spelling notebook 3x each that are wrong.	-CP4: p. 35 -SM: Take Post-test for grade.	
Grammar	-SJG4WB: p. 64		
Reading & Music		-SJSSB: Practice Gr. 4 songs #9-10, p. 32-33. Song files are on stjeromelibrary.org/music. Feel free to sing more songs of interest.	
History & Logic	-OWT: read p. 144-146 -OWTWB: p. 44-45		
Math	-SMTW4: Investigation 7	-SM4: L. 71 -SMTW4: Test H	
Science		-WND: p. 57-59	
Art & Geo-graphy	-SAA: teacher read p. 38-39 with student and discuss		

Subject	Monday	Tuesday	Wednesday
Religion			-LMR4: p. 220-226
Hand-writing & Spelling	-CP4: p. 36 -SM: p. 105-108, L. 18	-SM: p. 109-110	
Grammar	-SJG4: p. 167-172 (Stop at "Changing the Order of Words")	-SJG4WB: p. 65	-SJG4WB: p. 66
Reading & Music		-SJSR4: p. 358-367	-SJSR4: p. 368-372 (end!)
History & Logic		-OWT: read p. 149-152 -OWTWB: p. 46-47	
Math	-SM4: L. 72	-SM4: L. 73	-SM4: L. 74
Science		-SGW4: read p. 118-119 -SGW4WB: p. 45	-SGW4: read p. 120-123 -SGW4WB: p. 46
Art & Geo-graphy	-DKG4: p. 30		

Week 20

Week 20

Subject	Thursday	Friday	Comments
Religion			
Hand-writing & Spelling	-SM: Administer pre-test. Student writes words in Spelling notebook 3x each that are wrong.	-CP4: p. 37 -SM: Take Post-test for grade.	
Grammar	-SJG4WB: p. 67		
Reading & Music		-SJSSB: Practice Gr. 4 songs #9-10, p. 32-33. Song files are on stjeromelibrary.org/music. Feel free to sing more songs of interest.	
History & Logic	-OWT: read p. 152-156 -OWTWB: p. 48-49		
Math	-SM4: L. 75	-SMTW4: Test 14	
Science		-WND: p. 60-62	
Art & Geography	-SAA: teacher read p. 40-41 with student and discuss		

Week 21

Subject	Monday	Tuesday	Wednesday
Religion			-LMR4: p. 227-235
Hand-writing & Spelling	-CP4: p. 38 -SM: p. 111-114, L. 19	-SM: p. 115-116	
Grammar	-SJG4: p. 172-177 (Stop at "Correct Usage")	-SJG4WB: p. 68	-SJG4WB: p. 69
Reading & Music		-CW: p. 1-14	-CW: p. 15-24
History & Logic		-OWT: read p. 156-158 -OWTWB: p. 50	
Math	-SM4: L. 76	-SM4: L. 77	-SM4: L. 78
Science		-SGW4: read p. 124-126 -SGW4WB: p. 47	-SGW4: read p. 127-129 -SGW4WB: p. 48
Art & Geography	-DKG4: p. 31		

Subject	Thursday	Friday	Comments
Religion			
Hand-writing & Spelling	-SM: Administer pre-test. Student writes words in Spelling notebook 3x each that are wrong.	-CP4: p. 39 -SM: Take Post-test for grade.	
Grammar	-SJG4WB: p. 70-71		
Reading & Music		-SJSSB: Practice Gr. 4 songs #11-12, p. 34-35. Song files are on stjeromelibrary.org/music. Feel free to sing more songs of interest.	
History & Logic	-OWT: read p. 158-164	-OWTWB: p. 51-52	
Math	-SM4: L. 79	-SM4: L. 80	
Science		-WND: p. 63-64	
Art & Geography	-SAA: teacher read p. 42-43 with student and discuss		

Week 22

Subject	Monday	Tuesday	Wednesday
Religion			-LMR4: p. 236-241
Hand-writing & Spelling	-CP4: p. 40 -SM: p. 117-120, L. 20	-SM: p. 121-122	
Grammar	-SJG4: p. 177-180	-SJG4WB: p. 72	-SJG4WB: p. 73
Reading & Music		-CW: p. 25-36 (end!) What did student think? Is this new information or do they already know it? Have you made your 5*	-LT: p. v-5 (This book may be read with or without teacher)
History & Logic		-OWTWB: p. 53-54 (Review A-B)	
Math	-SMTW4: Test 15	-SM4: Investigation 8 -SMTW4: Activity Sheet 26	-SM4: L. 81
Science		-SGW4: read p. 130-132 -SGW4WB: p. 49	-SGW4: read p. 133-134 -SGW4WB: p. 50
Art & Geography	-DKG4: p. 32		

Week 22

Subject	Thursday	Friday	Comments
Religion			
Hand-writing & Spelling	-SM: Administer pre-test. Student writes words in Spelling notebook 3x each that are wrong.	-CP4: p. 41 -SM: Take Post-test for grade.	
Grammar	-SJG4WB: p. 74		
Reading & Music		-SJSSB: Practice Gr. 4 songs #11-12, p. 34-35. Song files are on stjeromelibrary.org/music. Feel free to sing more songs of interest.	*first Saturdays yet? Make plans to do so, if not. 😊
History & Logic	-OWTWB: p. 54-55 (Review C-E)		
Math	-SM4: L. 82	-SM4: L. 83	
Science		-WND: p. 65-66	
Art & Geography	-SAA: teacher read p. 44-45 with student and discuss		

Week 23

Subject	Monday	Tuesday	Wednesday
Religion			-LMR4: p. 242-251
Hand-writing & Spelling	-CP4: p. 42 -SM: p. 123-126, L. 21	-SM: p. 127-128	
Grammar	-SJG4: p. 181-184 (Stop at "Homonyms")	-SJG4WB: p. 75	-SJG4WB: p. 76
Reading & Music		-LT: p. 7-12	-LT: p. 13-18
History & Logic		-OWT: read p. 169-171 -OWTWB: p. 56-57	
Math	-SM4: L. 84	-SM4: L. 85	-SMTW4: Test 16
Science		-SGW4: read p. 135 -SGW4WB: p. 51	-SGW4: read p. 136-138 -SGW4WB: p. 52-53
Art & Geo-graphy	-DKG4: p. 33		

Week 23			
Subject	Thursday	Friday	Comments
Religion			
Hand-writing & Spelling	-SM: Administer pre-test. Student writes words in Spelling notebook 3x each that are wrong.	-CP4: p. 43 -SM: Take Post-test for grade.	
Grammar	-SJG4WB: p. 77		
Reading & Music		-SJSSB: Practice Gr. 4 songs #11-12, p. 34-35. Song files are on stjeromelibrary.org/music. Feel free to sing more songs of interest.	
History & Logic	-OWT: read p. 171-174	-OWTWB: p. 58-60	
Math	-SM4: L. 86	-SM4: L. 87	
Science		-WND: p. 67-68	
Art & Geography	-SAA: teacher read p. 46-47 with student and discuss		

Week 24

Subject	Monday	Tuesday	Wednesday
Religion			-LMR4: p. 252-260
Hand-writing & Spelling	-CP4: p. 44 -SM: p. 129-132, L. 22	-SM: p. 133-134	
Grammar	-SJG4: p. 184-189 (Stop at "Contractions")	-SJG4WB: p. 78	-SJG4WB: p. 79
Reading & Music		-LT: p. 19-26	-LT: p. 27-30
History & Logic		-OWT: read p. 177-181 -OWTWB: p. 61	
Math	-SM4: L. 88	-SM4: L. 89	-SM4: L. 90
Science		-SGW4: read p. 139-142 Do questions on p. 142 orally with teacher -SGW4WB: p. 54	-SGW4: read p. 143-147 -SGW4WB: p. 55
Art & Geography	-DKG4: p. 34		

	Week 24		
Subject	Thursday	Friday	Comments
Religion			
Hand-writing & Spelling	-SM: Administer pre-test. Student writes words in Spelling notebook 3x each that are wrong.	-CP4: p. 45 -SM: Take Post-test for grade.	
Grammar	-SJG4WB: p. 80		
Reading & Music		-SJSSB: Practice Gr. 4 songs #11-12, p. 34-35. Song files are on stjeromelibrary.org/music. Feel free to sing more songs of interest.	
History & Logic	-OWT: read p. 181-185		
Math	-SMTW4: Test 17	-SM4: Investigation 9 -SMTW4: Activity Sheets 28-30	
Science		-WND: p. 69-70	
Art & Geography	-SAA: teacher read p. 48-49 with student and discuss		

Week 25

Subject	Monday	Tuesday	Wednesday
Religion			-LMR4: p. 261-269
Hand-writing & Spelling	-CP4: p. 46 -SM: p. 135-138, L. 23	-SM: p. 139-140	
Grammar	-SJG4: p. 189-206 (Stop at "Polishing Paragraphs")	-SJG4WB: p. 81	-SJG4WB: p. 82
Reading & Music		-LT: p. 31-36	-LT: p. 37-41
History & Logic		-OWTWB: p. 62-63	
Math	-SM4: L. 91	-SM4: L. 92	-SM4: L. 93
Science		-SGW4: read p. 148-149 -SGW4WB: p. 56	-SGW4: read p. 150-152 -SGW4WB: p. 57
Art & Geography	-DKG4: p. 35		

Subject	Thursday	Friday	Comments
Religion			
Hand-writing & Spelling	-SM: Administer pre-test. Student writes words in Spelling notebook 3x each that are wrong.	-CP4: p. 47 -SM: Take Post-test for grade.	
Grammar	-SJG4WB: p. 83		
Reading & Music		-SJSSB: Practice Gr. 4 songs #13-14, p. 36-37. Song files are on stjeromelibrary.org/music. Feel free to sing more songs of interest.	
History & Logic	-OWT: read p. 188-190 -OWTWB: p. 64-65		
Math	-SM4: L. 94	-SM4: L. 95	
Science		-WND: p. 71-72	
Art & Geography	-SAA: teacher read p. 50-51 with student and discuss		

Week 25

Week 26

Subject	Monday	Tuesday	Wednesday
Religion			-LMR4: p. 270-278
Hand-writing & Spelling	-CP4: p. 48 -SM: p. 141-144, L. 24	-SM: p. 145-146	
Grammar	-SJG4: p. 206-218 (Stop at "Correct Usage")	-SJG4WB: p. 84-85	-SJG4WB: p. 86
Reading & Music		-LT: p. 43-47	-LT: p. 49-54
History & Logic		-OWT: read p. 190-193 -OWTWB: p. 66-67	
Math	-SMTW4: Test 18	-SM4: L. 96	-SM4: L. 97
Science		-SGW4: read p. 153-155 -SGW4WB: p. 58	-SGW4: read p. 156-157 -SGW4WB: p. 59
Art & Geography	-DKG4: p. 36		

Subject	Thursday	Friday	Comments
Religion			
Handwriting & Spelling	-SM: Administer pre-test. Student writes words in Spelling notebook 3x each that are wrong.	-CP4: p. 49 (end!) -SM: Take Post-test for grade.	
Grammar	-SJG4WB: p. 87		
Reading & Music		-SJSSB: Practice Gr. 4 songs #13-14, p. 36-37. Song files are on stjeromelibrary.org/music. Feel free to sing more songs of interest.	
History & Logic	-OWT: read p. 193-197	-OWTWB: p. 68-69	
Math	-SM4: L. 98	-SM4: L. 99	
Science		-WND: p. 73-74	
Art & Geography	-SAA: teacher read p. 52-53 with student and discuss		

Week 26

Week 27

Subject	Monday	Tuesday	Wednesday
Religion			
Handwriting & Spelling			
Grammar	-SJG4: p. 218-222 (Stop at "Word Study")	-SJG4WB: p. 88	-SJG4WB: p. 89
Reading & Music		-LT: p.55-62	-LT: p. 63-68
History & Logic		-OWT: Study for Third Quarter Exam (p. 141-197)	
Math	-SM4: L. 100 -SMTW4: Activity Sheets 31-33	-SMTW4: Test 19	-SM4: Investigation 10
Science		-SGW4: read p. 158-160 -SGW4WB: p. 60	-SGW4: read p. 161-163 -SGW4WB: p. 61
Art & Geography	-DKG4: p. 37		

Week 27			
Subject	Thursday	Friday	Comments
Religion			
Hand-writing & Spelling			
Grammar	-SJG4WB: p. 90		
Reading & Music		-SJSSB: Practice Gr. 4 songs #13-14, p. 36-37. Song files are on stjeromelibrary.org/music. Feel free to sing more songs of interest.	
History & Logic	-Third Quarter Exam Remove exam two pages from here.		
Math			
Science		-WND: p. 75-78	
Art & Geography			

Third Quarter History Exam
Old World Treasures
Grade 4

Name _____

Fill in the Blanks (some will not be used):

St. Augustine	America	St. Ambrose	monks & nuns
St. Patrick	Arabs	Red Sea	St. Monica
St. Genevieve	Pakistan	abbot	girls & boys
St. Anthony			

1. The Arabian Peninsula lies east of the _____.

2. The numbers that we use most frequently are called Arabic because they have come down to us from the _____ of the 8th and 9th centuries.

3. Christopher Columbus discovered _____ in 1492.

4. Men and women who wanted to spend their lives in prayer and penance to serve God alone were called _____.

5. In a monastery, all the monks obey their father, called an _____.

6. _____ was the first of the ancient monks.

7. The great _____ brought monastic life to northern Africa.

8. The mother of St. Augustine was _____.

9. St. Augustine was converted and baptized by _____.

10. _____ was the Apostle of the Irish.

In front of each of the items in Column B, write the number of the word or phrase in Column A which is most closely connected with it.

Column A	Column B
1. St. Patrick	( ) St. Benedict
2. a special school for priests	( ) Moravian Empire
3. Father of Western Monasticism	( ) St. Boniface
4. the king of Kent's wife	( ) St. Cyril & St. Methodius
5. the most important center of the Church of England	( ) Charlemagne
6. "Apostle of the Germans"	( ) Papal States
7. they preached to pagan Slavs	( ) Ireland
8. country of the Slavs was called	( ) Bertha, a Frankish princess
9. Charles the Great	( ) Canterbury
10. Rome and all the other places ruled by the Pope	( ) seminary

Circle yes if the statement is correct. Circle no if it is not correct.

yes   no   1. Charlemagne started the famous Palace School.

yes   no   2. The King of the Franks for 40 years was Charlemagne.

yes   no   3. Charlemagne was a very wise ruler. When he died in 814, his subjects were very sad.

yes   no   4. The barbarians came from Rome.

yes   no   5. The name given to the period of history between 476 and 1492 is the Middle Ages.

yes   no   6. Charlemagne's bloodiest wars were fought against the Normans.

yes   no   7. Lotharingia was ruled by the Pope.

yes   no   8. Alfred the Great became King of the Danes.

yes   no   9. William, Duke of Normandy, invaded and conquered Italy.

yes   no   10. Great stone houses in feudal times were called castles.

yes   no   11. The part of a castle which was a place of special safety was called the tower.

yes   no   12. A moat was a wandering singer.

yes   no   13. Material used to make armor in feudal times was called mail.

yes   no   14. Ditches dug around castle walls for safety were called accolades.

yes   no   15. Chivalry was called the Knightly Code of Manners.

Week 28

Subject	Monday	Tuesday	Wednesday
Religion			-LMR4: p. 279-285
Hand-writing & Spelling	-SM: p. 147-150, L. 25	-SM: p. 151-152	
Grammar	-SJG4: p. 222-226 (Stop at "Other Homonyms")	-SJG4WB: p. 91	-SJG4WB: p. 92
Reading & Music		-LT: p. 69-74	-LT: p. 75-79
History & Logic		-OWT: read p. 200-204 -OWTWB: p. 70	
Math	-SM4: L. 101	-SM4: L. 102	-SM4: L. 103
Science		-SGW4: read p. 164-167 -SGW4WB: p. 62	-SGW4: read p. 168-174 Do questions on p. 174 orally with teacher -SGW4WB: p. 63
Art & Geography	-DKG4: p. 38		

Week 28

Subject	Thursday	Friday	Comments
Religion			
Hand-writing & Spelling	-SM: Administer pre-test. Student writes words in Spelling notebook 3x each that are wrong.	-SM: Take Post-test for grade.	
Grammar	-SJG4WB: p. 93		
Reading & Music		-SJSSB: Practice Gr. 4 songs #13-14, p. 36-37. Song files are on stjeromelibrary.org/music. Feel free to sing more songs of interest.	
History & Logic	-OWT: read p. 204-209 -OWTWB: p. 71-72		
Math	-SM4: L. 104	-SM4: L. 105	
Science		-WND: p. 79-81 Grade for extra credit, but child should complete.	
Art & Geo-graphy	-SAA: teacher read p. 54-55 with student and discuss		

Week 29

Subject	Monday	Tuesday	Wednesday
Religion			-LMR4: p. 286-296
Hand-writing & Spelling	-SM: p. 153-156, L. 26	-SM: p. 157-158	
Grammar	-SJG4: p. 226-231 (Stop at "Capital Letters")	-SJG4WB: p. 94	-SJG4WB: p. 95
Reading & Music		-LT: p. 81-89	-LT: p. 91-96
History & Logic		-OWTWB: p. 73-74 (Review A-C)	
Math	-SMTW4: Test 20	-SM4: L. 106	-SM4: L. 107
Science		-SGW4: read p. 175-177 -SGW4WB: p. 64	-SGW4: read p. 178-181 -SGW4WB: p. 65
Art & Geography	-DKG4: p. 39		

Week 29

Subject	Thursday	Friday	Comments
Religion			
Hand-writing & Spelling	-SM: Administer pre-test. Student writes words in Spelling notebook 3x each that are wrong.	-SM: Take Post-test for grade.	
Grammar	-SJG4WB: p. 96		
Reading & Music		-SJSSB: Practice Gr. 4 songs #15-17, p. 38-41. Song files are on stjeromelibrary.org/music. Feel free to sing more songs of interest.	
History & Logic	-OWTWB: p. 74-76 (Review D-E)		
Math	-SM4: L. 108	-SM4: L. 109	
Science		-WND: p. 82 Experiment	
Art & Geography	-SAA: teacher read p. 56-57 with student and discuss		

Week 30

Subject	Monday	Tuesday	Wednesday
Religion			-LMR4: p. 297-306
Hand-writing & Spelling	-SM: p. 159-162, L. 27	-SM: p. 163-164	
Grammar	-SJG4: p. 231-239 (end!)	-SJG4WB: p. 97	-SJG4WB: p. 98
Reading & Music		-LT: p. 97-103	-LT: p. 105-108
History & Logic		-OWT: read p. 212-215	
Math	-SM4: L. 110	-SMTW4: Test 21	-SM4: Investigation 11
Science		-SGW4: read p. 182-183 -SGW4WB: p. 66	-SGW4: read p. 184-189 -SGW4WB: p. 67
Art & Geography	-DKG4: p. 40	-DKG4: p. 41	

Week 30

Subject	Thursday	Friday	Comments
Religion			
Hand-writing & Spelling	-SM: Administer pre-test. Student writes words in Spelling notebook 3x each that are wrong.	-SM: Take Post-test for grade.	
Grammar	-SJG4WB: p. 99		
Reading & Music		-SJSSB: Practice Gr. 4 songs #15-17, p. 38-41. Song files are on stjeromelibrary.org/music. Feel free to sing more songs of interest.	
History & Logic	-OWTWB: p. 77-79		
Math	-SM4: L. 111 -SMTW4: Activity Sheet 35	-SM4: L. 112	
Science		-WND: p. 83	
Art & Geography	-SAA: teacher read p. 58-59 with student and discuss		

Week 31

Subject	Monday	Tuesday	Wednesday
Religion			-LMR4: p. 307-314
Hand-writing & Spelling	-SM: p. 165-168, L. 28	-SM: p. 169-170	
Grammar	-SJG4WB: p. 100 Test (end!)		
Reading & Music		-LT: p. 109-115	-LT: p. 117-122
History & Logic		-OWT: read p. 215-218 -OWTWB: p. 80-81	
Math	-SM4: L. 113	-SM4: L. 114	-SM4: L. 115
Science		-SGW4: read p. 190-191 -SGW4WB: p. 68	-SGW4: read p. 192-194 -SGW4WB: p. 69
Art & Geography	-Remove Map #1 from the back. Give to student to study states.*	-DKG4: p. 42	

Week 31

Subject	Thursday	Friday	Comments
Religion			
Hand-writing & Spelling	-SM: Administer pre-test. Student writes words in Spelling notebook 3x each that are wrong.	-SM: Take Post-test for grade.	
Grammar			
Reading & Music		-SJSSB: Practice Gr. 4 songs #15-17, p. 38-41. Song files are on stjeromelibrary.org/music. Feel free to sing more songs of interest.	
History & Logic	-OWT: read p. 221-229	-OWTWB: p. 82-83	
Math	-SMTW4: Test 22	-SM4: L. 116	
Science		-WND: p. 84-85	
Art & Geography	-SAA: teacher read p. 60-61 with student and discuss		*Show student the list for the test and Map #2 so he knows what to expect on next Monday.

Week 32

Subject	Monday	Tuesday	Wednesday
Religion			-LMR4: p. 315-324 (Stop at "The Resurrection of the Body")
Hand-writing & Spelling	-SM: p. 171-174, L. 29	-SM: p. 175-176	
Grammar			
Reading & Music		-LT: p. 123-126	-LT: p. 127-132
History & Logic		-OWT: read p. 232-235	
Math	-SM4: L. 117	-SM4: L. 118	-SM4: L. 119
Science		-SGW4: read p. 195-198 (end!) Do questions orally with teacher on p. 198 -SGW4WB: p. 70 (end!)	
Art & Geography	-Give test with Map #2 and List. This could be just for fun or grade.	-DKG4: p. 43	

Week 32

Subject	Thursday	Friday	Comments
Religion			
Hand-writing & Spelling	-SM: Administer pre-test. Student writes words in Spelling notebook 3x each that are wrong.	-SM: Take Post-test for grade.	
Grammar			
Reading & Music		-SJSSB: Practice Gr. 4 songs #15-17, p. 38-41. Song files are on stjeromelibrary.org/music. Feel free to sing more songs of interest.	
History & Logic	-OWTWB: p. 84-85		
Math	-SM4: L. 120	-SMTW4: Test 23	
Science		-WND: p. 86-88	
Art & Geography	-SAA: teacher read p. 62-63 with student and discuss		

Week 33

Subject	Monday	Tuesday	Wednesday
Religion			-LMR4: p. 324-331 (end!)
Hand-writing & Spelling	-SM: p. 177-180, L. 30	-SM: p. 181-182	
Grammar			
Reading & Music		-LT: p. 133-139	-LT: p. 141-152
History & Logic		-OWT: read p. 235-237	
Math	-SM4: Investigation 12 -SMTW4: Activity Sheet 36	-SM4: p. 561 Topic A	-SM4: p. 563, Topic B
Science		-For the rest of the year, do some exploring outside and research some of what the student may find.	
Art & Geography	-Remove Map #3 from the back. Give to student to study.*	-DKG4: p. 44	

Week 33

Subject	Thursday	Friday	Comments
Religion			
Hand-writing & Spelling	-SM: Administer pre-test. Student writes words in Spelling notebook 3x each that are wrong.	-SM: Take Post-test for grade.	
Grammar			
Reading & Music		-SJSSB: Practice Gr. 4 songs #18-20, p. 42-44. Song files are on stjeromelibrary.org/music. Feel free to sing more songs of interest.	
History & Logic	-OWTWB: p. 86-87		
Math	-SM4: p. 565, Topic C		
Science		-WND: p. 89-93	
Art & Geography			*Show student the list for the test and Map #4 so he knows what to expect on next Monday.

Week 34

Subject	Monday	Tuesday	Wednesday
Religion			
Hand-writing & Spelling	-SM: p. 183-186, L. 31	-SM: p. 187-188	
Grammar			
Reading & Music		-LT: p. 153-163	-LT: p. 165-174 (Stop at "A Young Girl…")
History & Logic		-OWT: read p. 241-245	-OWTWB: p. 88-89
Math			
Science	-WND: Keep those weather records going.		
Art & Geography	-Give test with Map #4 and List. This could be just for fun or grade.	-DKG4: p. 45	

Subject	Thursday	Friday	Comments
Religion			
Handwriting & Spelling	-SM: Administer pre-test. Student writes words in Spelling notebook 3x each that are wrong.	-SM: Take Post-test for grade.	
Grammar			
Reading & Music		-SJSSB: Practice Gr. 4 songs #18-20, p. 42-44. Song files are on stjeromelibrary.org/music. Feel free to sing more songs of interest.	
History & Logic	-OWT: read p. 245-249	-OWTWB: p. 90	
Math			
Science		-WND: p. 94-96	
Art & Geography			

Week 34

Week 35

Subject	Monday	Tuesday	Wednesday
Religion			
Hand-writing & Spelling	-SM: p. 189-192, L. 32	-SM: p. 193-194	
Grammar			
Reading & Music		-LT: p. 174-183	-LT: p. 184-196 (end!)
History & Logic		-OWTWB: p. 91-92 (Review A-C)	
Math			
Science	-WND: Keep those weather records going.		
Art & Geography		-DKG4: p. 46	

Week 35

Subject	Thursday	Friday	Comments
Religion			
Hand-writing & Spelling	-SM: Administer pre-test. Student writes words in Spelling notebook 3x each that are wrong.	-SM: Take Post-test for grade. (end!)	
Grammar			
Reading & Music		-SJSSB: Practice Gr. 4 songs #18-20, p. 42-44. Song files are on stjeromelibrary.org/music. Feel free to sing more songs of interest.	
History & Logic	-OWTWB: p. 93-94 (end!) (Review D-F)		
Math			
Science		-WND: p. 97-98	
Art & Geography			

Week 36

Subject	Monday	Tuesday	Wednesday
Religion			
Hand-writing & Spelling			
Grammar			
Reading & Music	-MM: Read p. 1-17		-MM: Read p. 18-34 (end!) Discuss this graphic novel with your child. What did he think of it? What should we remember?
History & Logic		-OWT: Study for Fourth Quarter Exam (p. 200-253)	
Math			
Science	-WND: Keep those weather records going.		
Art & Geography		-DKG4: p. 47 (end!)	

Week 36

Subject	Thursday	Friday	Comments
Religion			
Hand-writing & Spelling			
Grammar			
Reading & Music		-SJSSB: Practice Gr. 4 songs #18-20, p. 42-44. Song files are on stjeromelibrary.org/music. Feel free to sing more songs of interest.	
History & Logic	-Fourth Quarter Exam Remove exam two pages from here.		
Math			
Science		-WND: p. 17. Look over all the completed months of weather records to answer the questions. Show the records to your parents*	*and explain observations made.
Art & Geography		-Eat a bowl of ice cream and maybe give the student one, too! 😉	

Quarter History Exam

Old World Treasures

Grade 4

Name _____

Fill in the Blanks (some will not be used):

merchants	Crusades	Italy	Turks
knights	Turks	Marco Polo	guilds
Venice	Joseph	Rome	children

1. Business men in the Middle Ages were called _____.

2. The _____ of the Middle Ages protected the merchants.

3. Venice was a very important trading city in northern _____.

4. While in prison, _____ wrote a book about all his wonderful travels called "The Travels of Marco Polo."

5. Marco Polo was born in the city of _____.

6. The _____ were really holy wars which were fought by Christians of western Europe to get back the Holy Land.

7. Pope Urban II asked the Christians to fight against the _____; this was known as the First Crusade.

8. The first real crusade was led by _____.

9. Kings and even _____ joined the crusades.

10. Saracens is another name for the _____.

In front of each of the items in Column B, write the number of the word or phrase in Column A which is most closely connected with it.

Column A   Column B

1. battle cry of the Crusades   ( ) John Gutenberg
2. great leader of the Turks   ( ) Michelangelo
3. king of England who joined a crusade   ( ) Richard the Lion-hearted
4. king of France who went on the Third crusade   ( ) Frederick Barbarossa
5. king that drowned in Asia Minor   ( ) Godfrey of Bouillon
6. took the title "Defender of the Holy Sepulcher" ( ) Saladin
7. preached the Second Crusade   ( ) St. Dominic
8. forbade fighting during Lent & Advent   ( ) St. Thomas Aquinas
9. known as the Angelic Doctor   ( ) The Truce of God
10. founded the Order of Preachers   ( ) "God wills it"
11. Renaissance sculptor   ( ) St. Bernard
12. invented the printing press   ( ) Philip Augustus

Circle yes if the statement is correct. Circle no if it is not correct.

- yes   no   1. The English king's son Edward is known as the White Prince because of the color of his armor.
- yes   no   2. During the Hundred Years' War, a terrible disease called the "Black Death" killed almost half of the population of Europe.
- yes   no   3. Joan of Arc led the English armies to victory.
- yes   no   4. Prince Charles was a Portuguese navigator who gave all his time and money to start a school for navigators.
- yes   no   5. Ferdinand and Isabella were king and queen of Spain in 1492.
- yes   no   6. The English were cruel to Joan of Arc.
- yes   no   7. Raphael was the favorite painter of the pope of his time.
- yes   no   8. Dante wrote a great work called "The Adoration of the Shepherds."
- yes   no   9. The compass and astrolabe helped pave the way to new lands during the Renaissance.
- yes   no   10. Leonardo da Vinci painted the frescoes on the ceiling of the Sistine Chapel.
- yes   no   11. The Renaissance is the bridge between the Middle Ages and modern times.
- yes   no   12. During the Middle Ages the people wrote on parchment which is the skin of sheep or goats treated in a special way to make it smooth.

yes **no** 13. The mother of St. Augustine was St. Helena.

yes **no** 14. A ditch dug around castle walls for safety was called a moat.

yes **no** 15. Charlemagne was a very wise ruler. When he died in 814, his subjects were very sad.

ST. JEROME SCHOOL

Grade 4 Report Card for the _____ AD- _____ AD School Year

Student's Name _____

Subject	1st Quarter	2nd Quarter	3rd Quarter	4th Quarter	Final Grade
Religion					
Handwriting				-----	
Spelling					
Grammar					
Reading					
Music					
Logic			-----	-----	
History					
Math					
Science					
Art					
Geography					

PERCENTAGE TO LETTER GRADE CONVERSION

LETTER	A+	A	A-	B+	B	B-	C+
%	97%-100%	93-96%	90%-92%	87%-89%	83%-86%	80%-82%	77%-79%
LETTER	C	C-	D+	D	D-	F	
%	73%-76%	70%-72%	67%-69%	63%-66%	60%-62%	0%-59%	

Notes from Teacher

1st Quarter _____

_____

2nd Quarter _____

_____

3rd Quarter _____

_____

4th Quarter _____

_____

Parent's Signature _____

United States of America

Map #1

Map #2

United States of America

List of United States for Map #2 Test

Alabama
Alaska
Arizona
Arkansas
California
Colorado
Connecticut
Delaware
Florida
Georgia
Hawaii
Idaho
Illinois
Indiana
Iowa
Kansas
Kentucky
Louisiana
Maine
Maryland
Massachusetts
Michigan
Minnesota
Mississippi
Missouri
Montana

Nebraska
Nevada
New Hampshire
New Jersey
New Mexico
New York
North Carolina
North Dakota
Ohio
Oklahoma
Oregon
Pennsylvania
Rhode Island
South Carolina
South Dakota
Tennessee
Texas
Utah
Vermont
Virginia
Washington
West Virginia
Wisconsin
Wyoming

North America
List of Countries and Bodies of Water for Map #4

Arctic Ocean
Atlantic Ocean
Baffin Bay
Bearfort Sea
Belize
Canada
Caribbean Sea
Cuba
El Salvador
Greenland
Guatemala
Gulf of Mexico
Honduras
Hudson Bay
Iceland
Jamaica
Labrador Sea
Mexico
Pacific Ocean
United States of America (USA)

SJS Book Report

Book Title:

Author:

Student Name:

Grade:

Submission Date:

Plot (what happened)

Characters

Themes (Main Idea)

Conflicts and Resolutions

Favorite event

Personal Impressions